The Cell and Division Biology for Kids

CHILDREN'S BIOLOGY BOOKS

BABY PROFESSOR

EDUCATION KIDS

Speedy Publishing LLC

40 E. Main St. #1156

Newark, DE 19711

www.speedypublishing.com

Copyright 2016

What are we made up of? All organisms are amazingly created. Human beings, for example, contain structures that help them survive and stay alive.

What could these structures be? Read on and learn the most amazing structure of life. Let's explore and talk about cells.

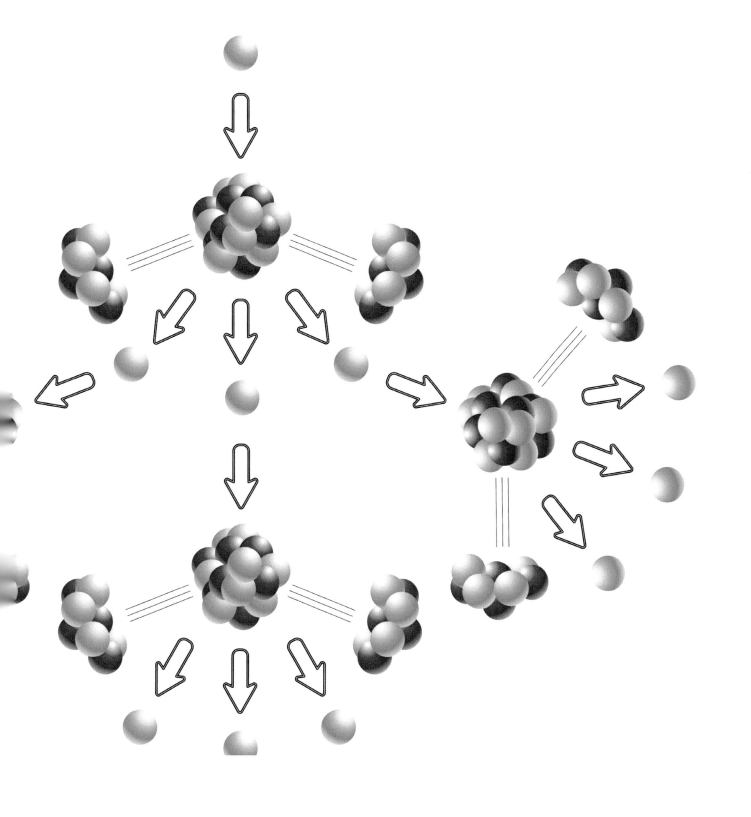

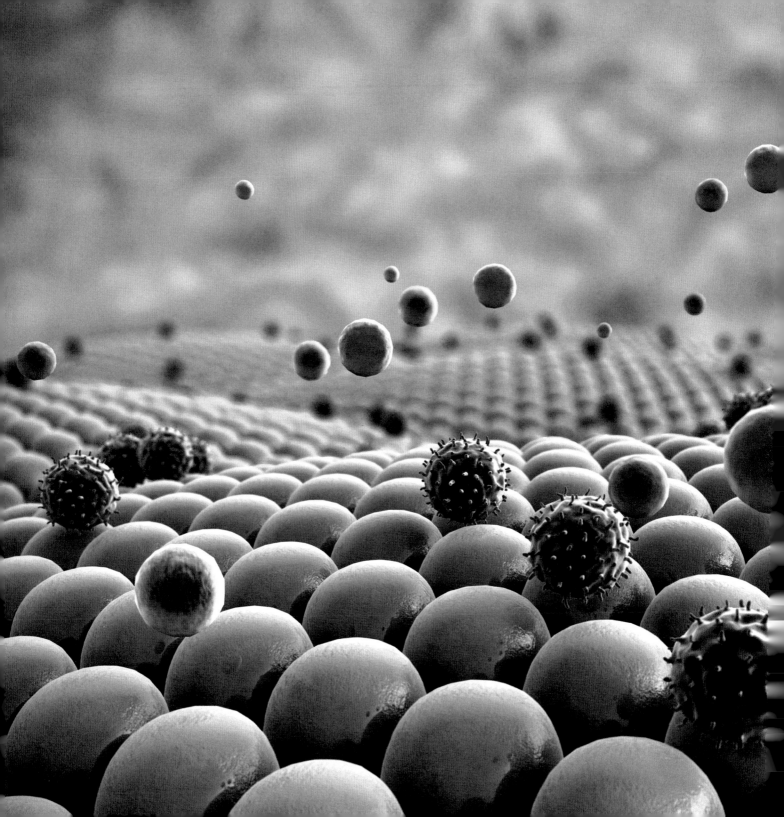

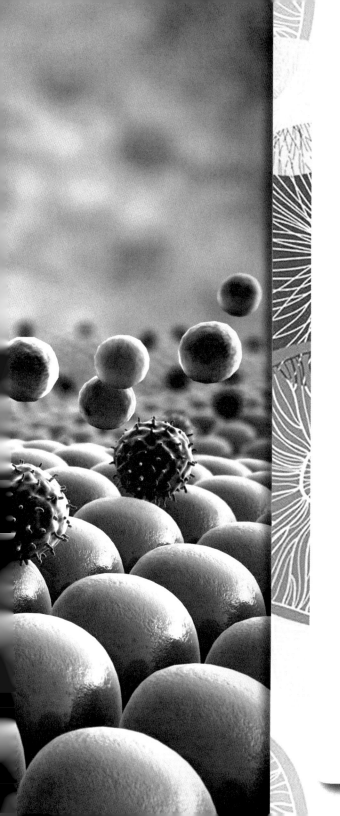

WHAT ARE CELLS?

Cells are the basic units of life. They are the basic building blocks of life. Interestingly, all living things on Earth are made up of cells. This is indicated in the study called biology.

All living organisms depend on cells to function normally. Organisms could contain one cell or millions of them. We call them unicellular or multicellular life forms. In fact, our body is estimated to be a world of approximately 100 trillion cells.

Our body has different types of cells. Cells help organisms function well by making them stable. Cells provide our body with an amazing structure which give us energy to live and reproduce.

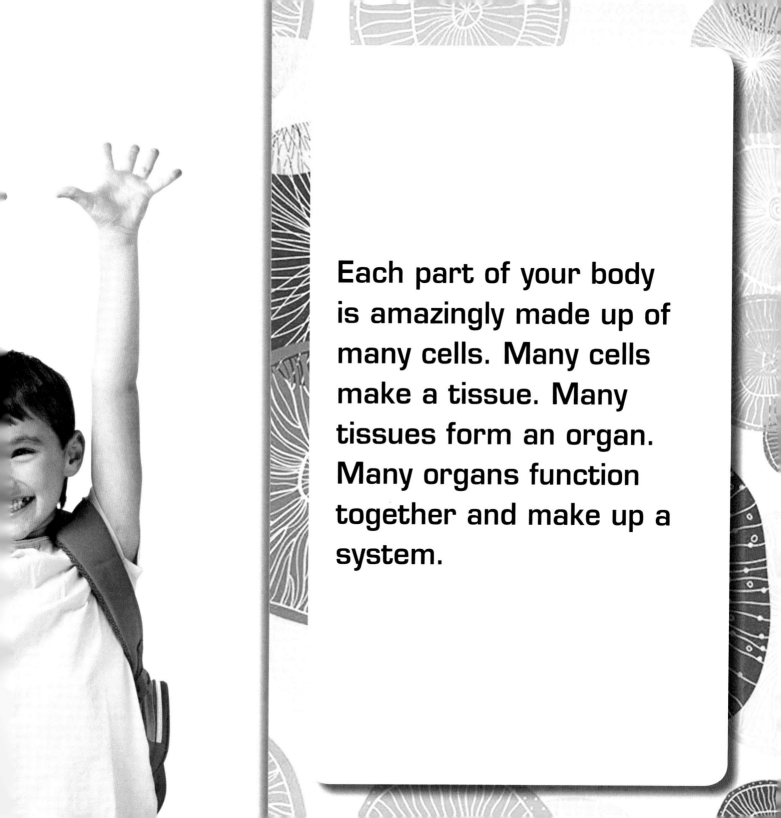

Each part of your body is amazingly made up of many cells. Many cells make a tissue. Many tissues form an organ. Many organs function together and make up a system.

This is the amazing human body! As you can see, we are basically composed of the tiny structures called cells.

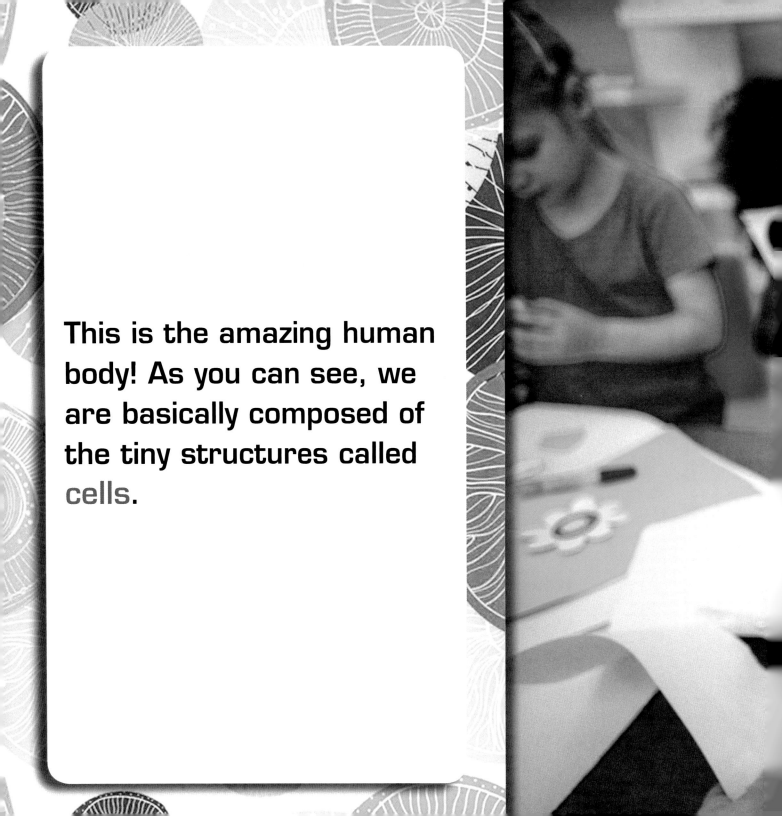

DID YOU KNOW THAT OUR BODY HAS MORE BACTERIAL CELLS THAN HUMAN CELLS?

According to scientists, the human body contains an estimated 95% bacterial cells of which most are found in the digestive tract.

Each cell has different functions. Red blood cells move through the blood system throughout the body and carry oxygen and nutrients for the body to function well. They are created inside the bone marrow of the bones.

Muscle cells stay together in bundles or sheets. Skin cells are capable of dividing and reproducing very quickly while nerve cells divide and reproduce only when necessary.

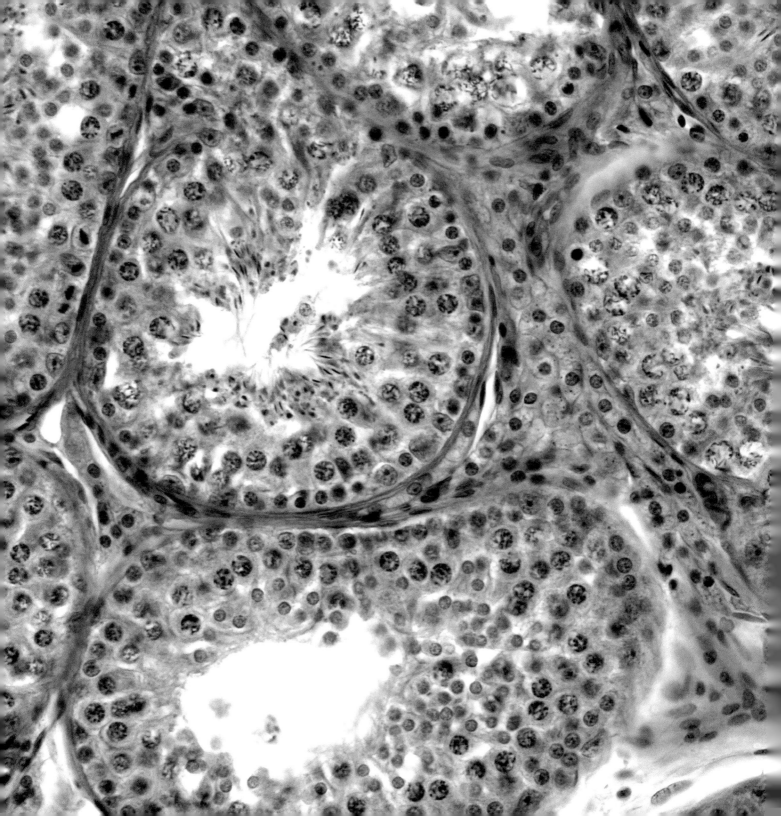

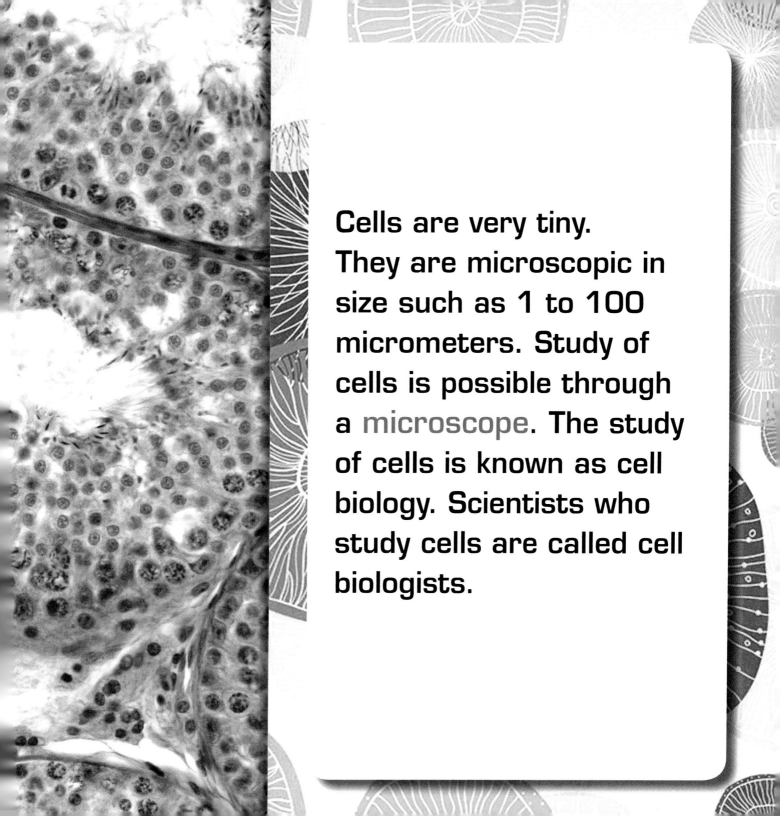

Cells are very tiny. They are microscopic in size such as 1 to 100 micrometers. Study of cells is possible through a microscope. The study of cells is known as cell biology. Scientists who study cells are called cell biologists.

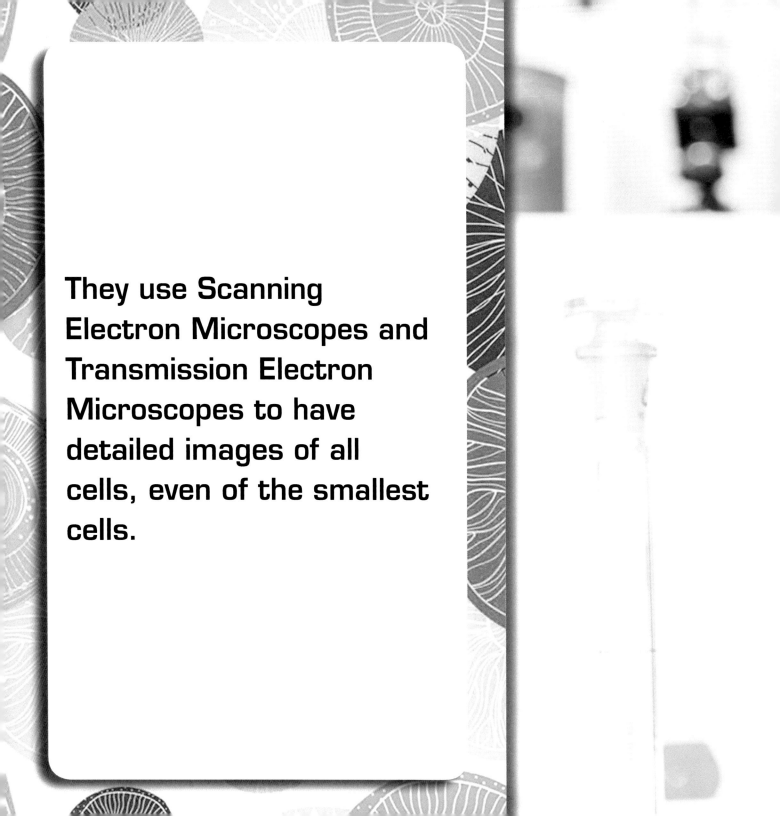

They use Scanning Electron Microscopes and Transmission Electron Microscopes to have detailed images of all cells, even of the smallest cells.

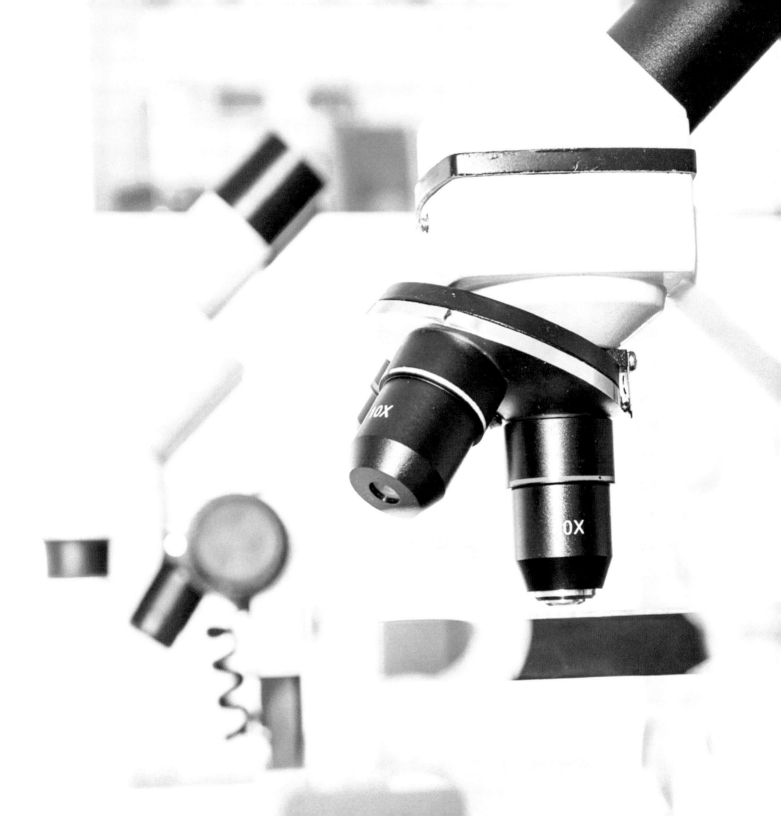

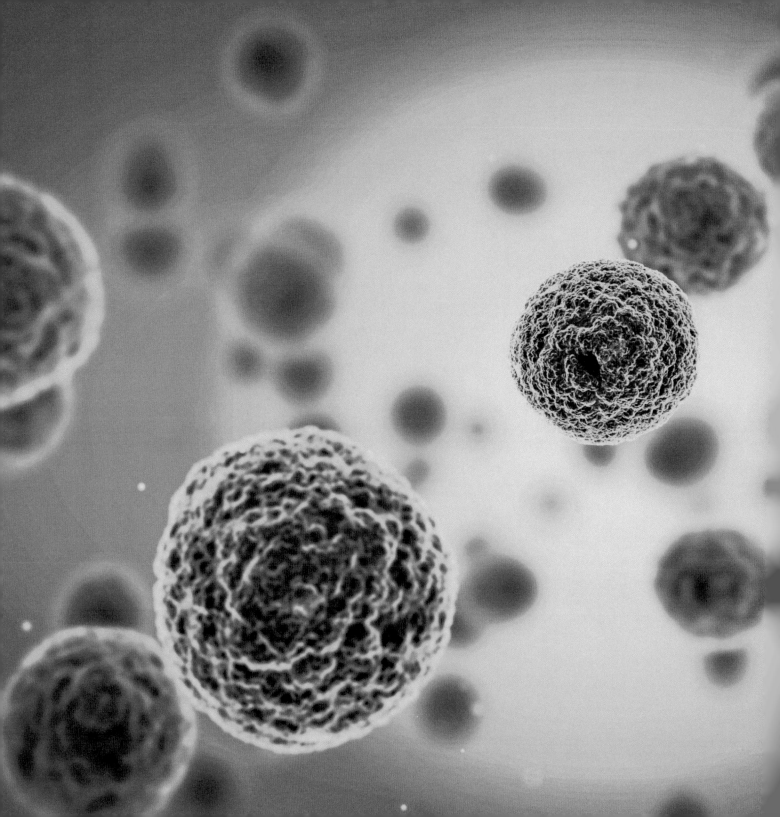

This is how technology works! We come to know everything, the mysterious and the unknown and the smallest of all structures!

The motor neurons are considered as the longest cells in the human body. These cells can grow up to 1.37 meters long. They extend from the lower spinal cord to the toes.

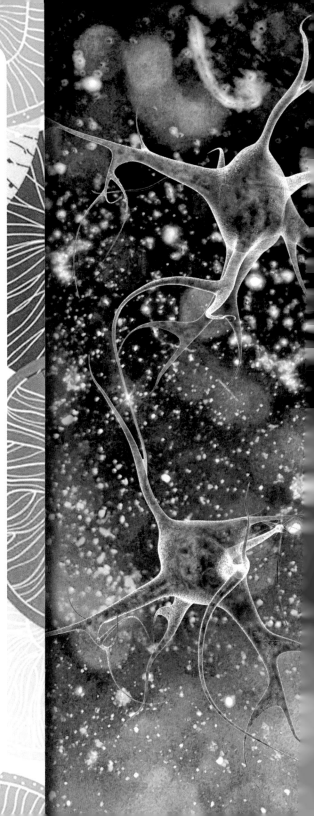

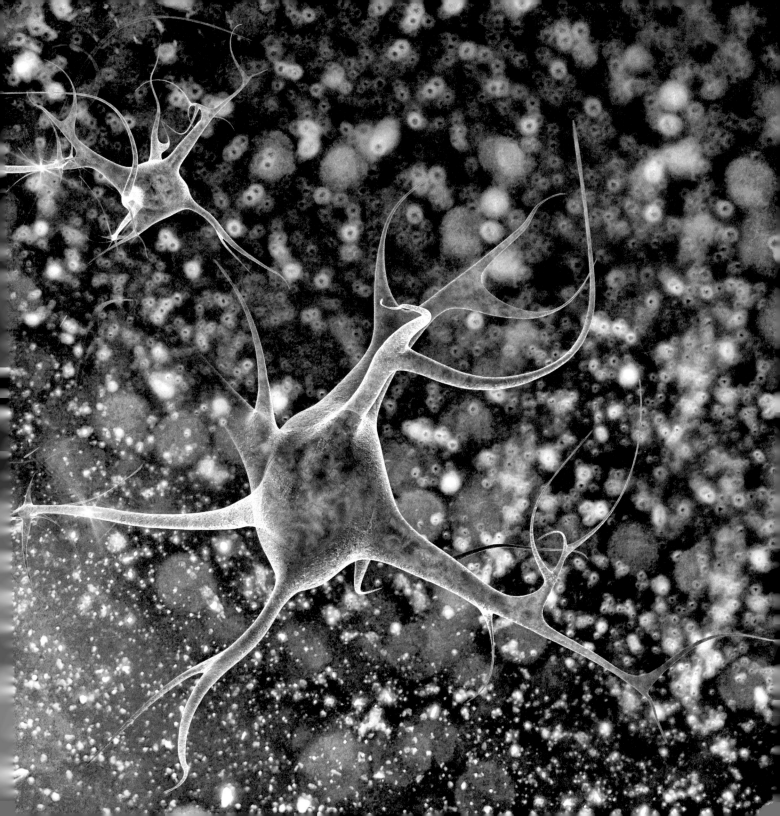

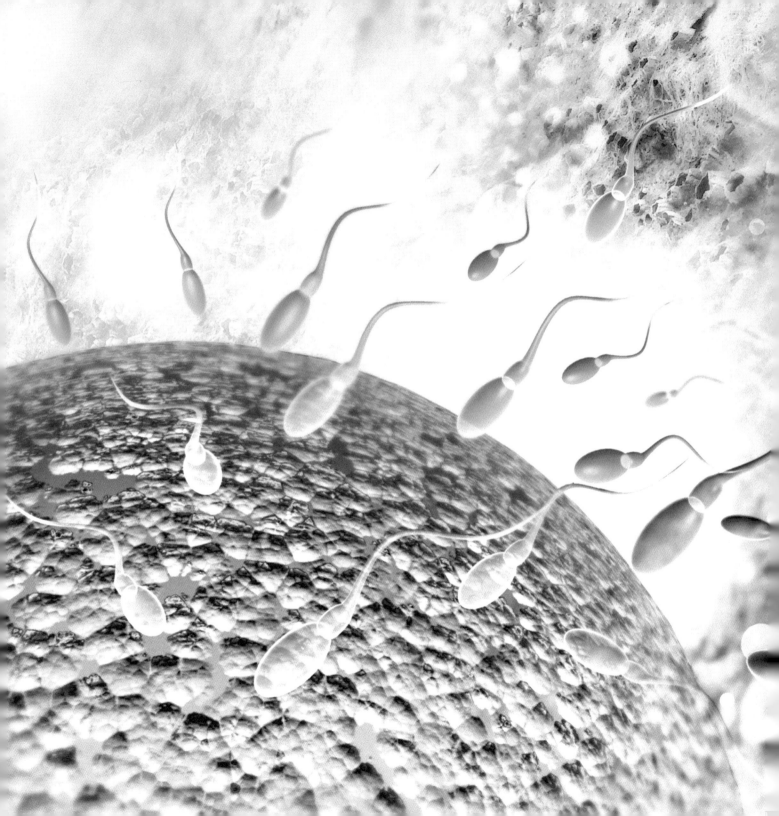

A fertilized egg is considered as the largest cell, yet it still so tiny that it can't be seen with the naked eye.

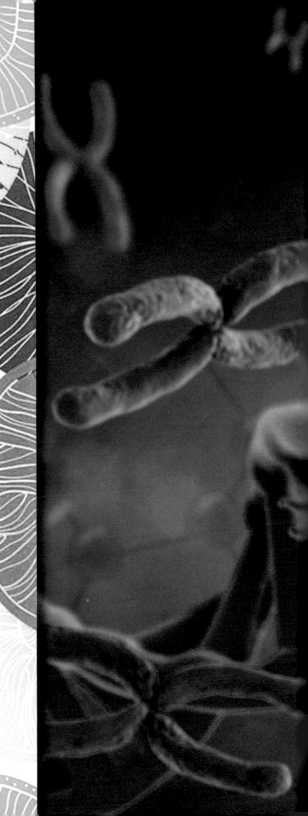

According to cell biologists, a human cell is normally composed of 46 chromosomes. Cells in people diagnosed with Down's Syndrome contain 47 chromosomes.

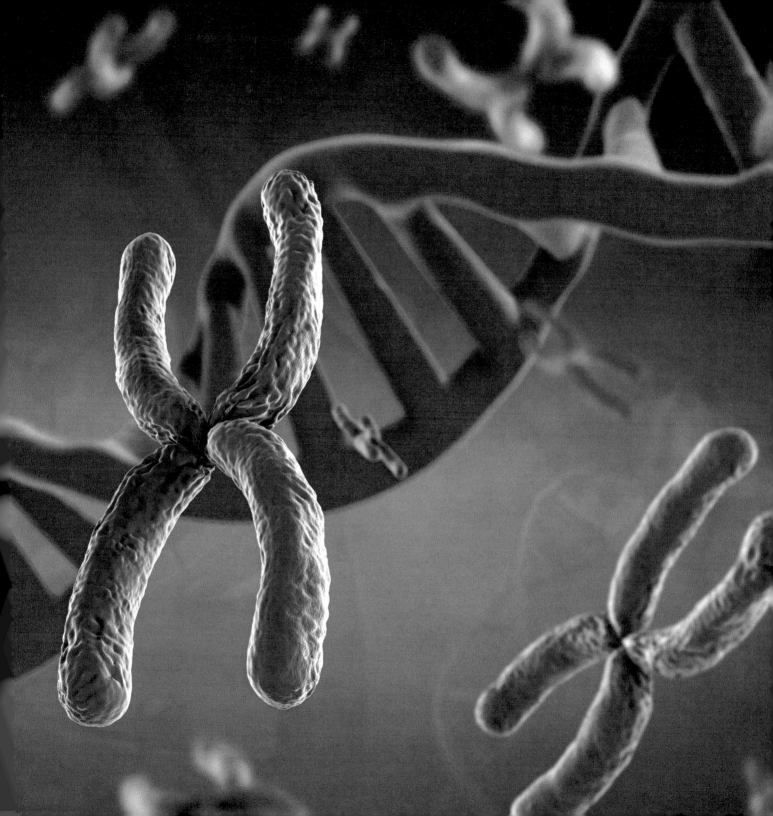

Did you know that the ostrich egg is the biggest cell in the whole world? It is so big that we have to use two hands to pick it up.

WHAT ARE THE TWO MAIN TYPES OF CELLS?

➲ **Eukaryotic**
➲ **Prokaryotik**

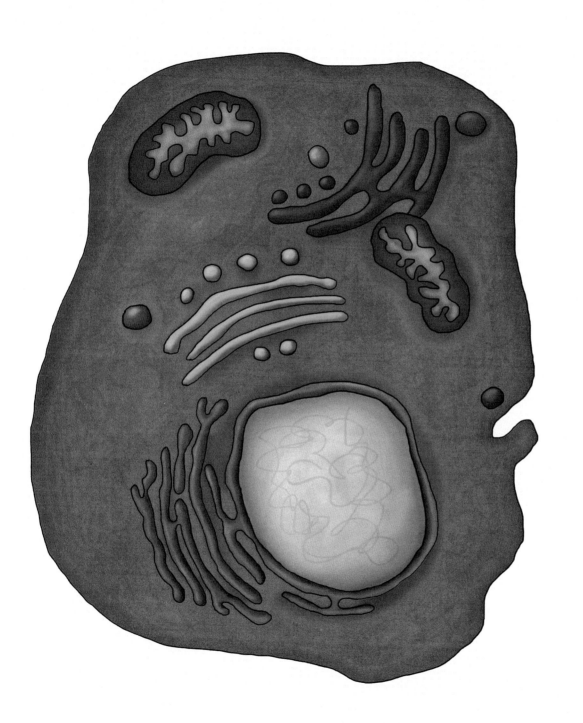

Eukaryotic cells

These cells contain a real nucleus. Their nucleus is what makes them ten times larger than prokaryotic cells. Examples of organisms with eukaryotic cells are plants, animals, and fungi.

Prokaryotic Cells

These cells are known to be the earliest forms of life in the universe. They are found in single-celled organisms such as bacteria and archaeans.

Prokaryotes are capable of surviving even in extreme habitats. They can survive in deadly environments. Archaeans can survive in hot and wet environments and even in animal intestines.

Bacteria Cell Anatomy

pilus

ribosome

capsule

cell wall

flagellum

nucleoid (DNA)

cell membrane

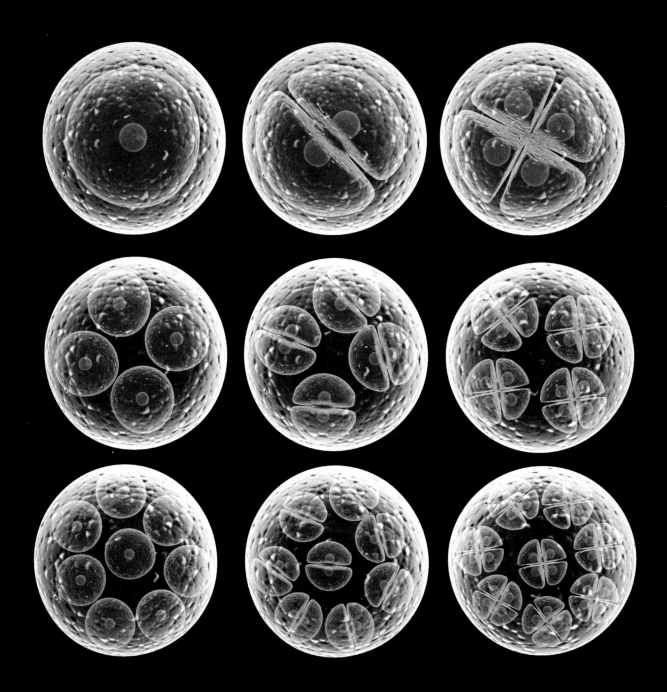

WHAT IS CELL DIVISION?

It is the basic feature or characteristic of life. Cell division is the process of making new cells. It is the process by which a parent cell is divided into two daughter cells.

It is amazing to know that when the parent cell divides, everything it has also divides. Living organisms continue to make up new cells as replacements to old and worn-out cells.

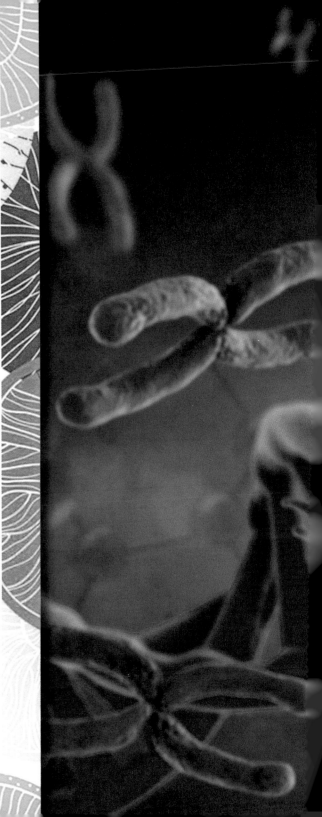

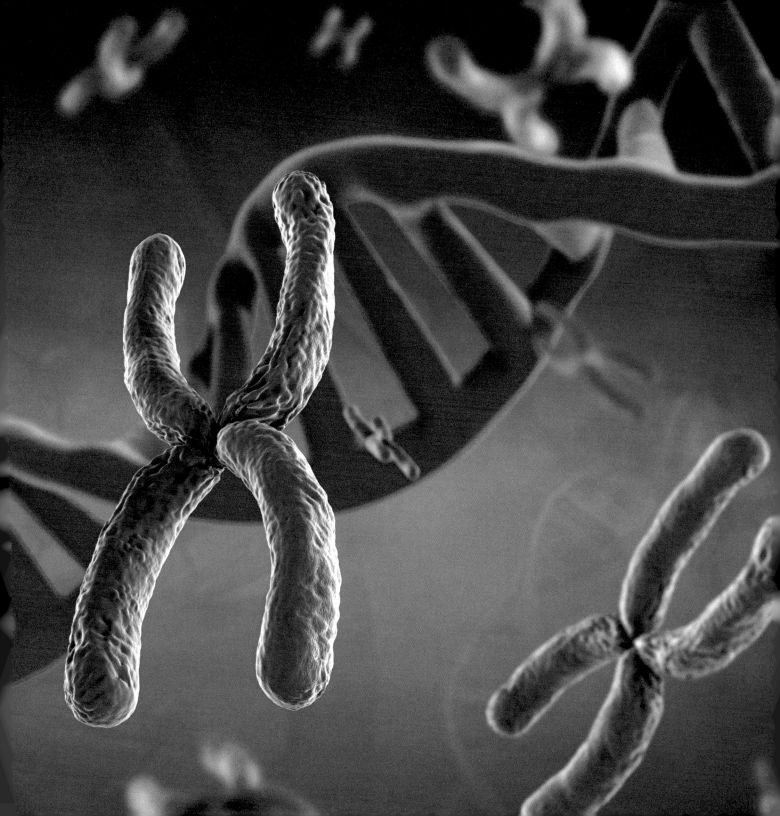

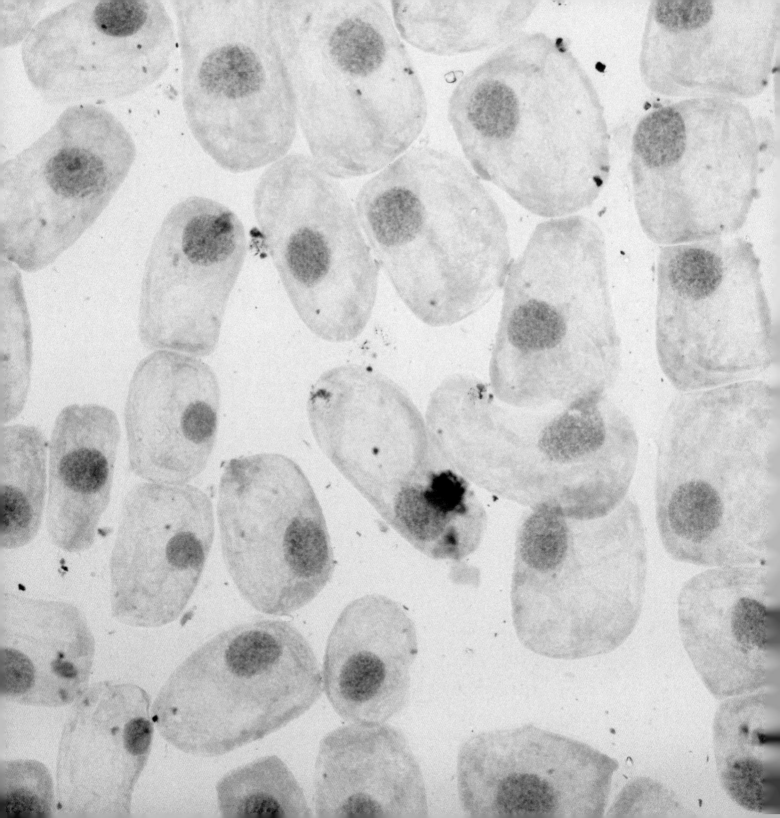

HERE ARE THE THREE TYPES OF CELL DIVISION.

- ➲ Binary Fission
- ➲ Mitosis
- ➲ Meiosis

1. Binary Fission

It is cell division of single-celled organisms such as bacteria. It is used by prokaryotic cells.

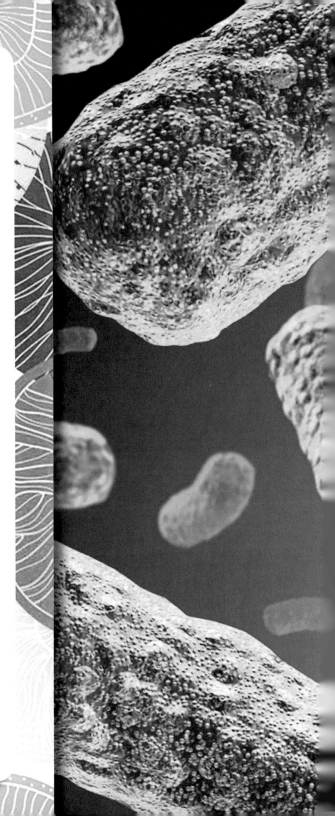

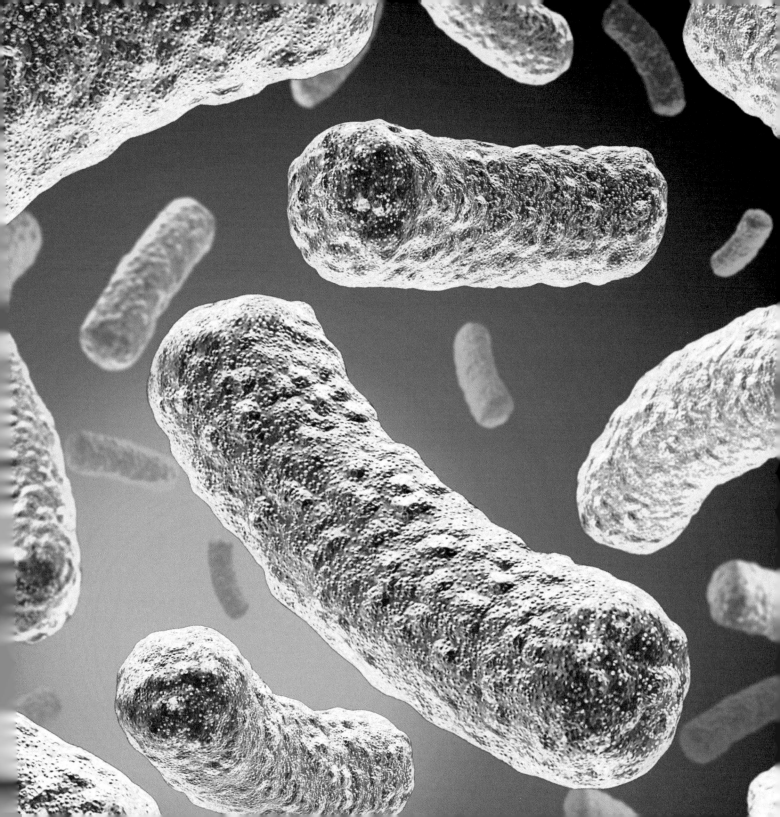

Cell division (mitosis)

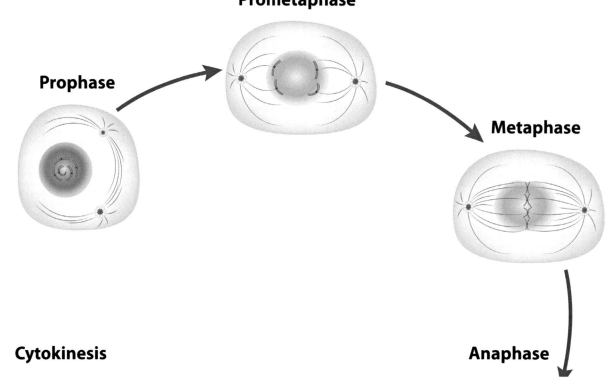

Prophase

Prometaphase

Metaphase

Anaphase

Cytokinesis

2. Mitosis

This happens when a mother cell is duplicated or divided to make two daughter cells which are exact copies of it. Everything in the cell is duplicated.

The newly formed cells have exactly the same functions, DNA, and genetic code. Our skin cells, blood cells, and muscle cells are produced through mitosis.

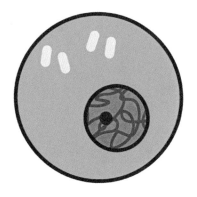

INTERPHASE

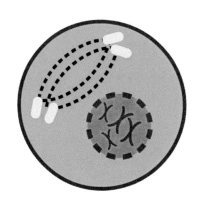

PROPHASE

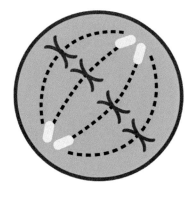

METAPHASE

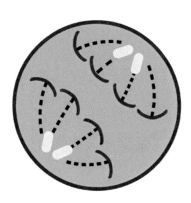

ANAPHASE

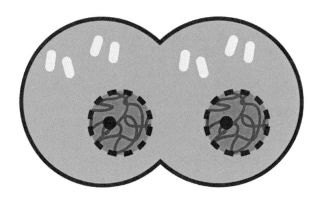

TELOPHASE

DAUGHTER
CELLS

The cells undergo a cell cycle which involves amazing stages namely, interphase, prophase, metaphase, anaphase, and telophase.

Cytokinesis or cell cleavage is the process splitting of the cells. Mitosis produces diploids which are cells with two complete sets of chromosomes.

Cell division (meiosis)

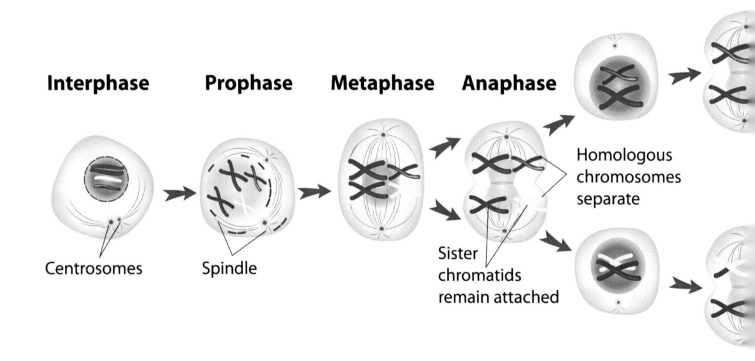

Interphase **Prophase** **Metaphase** **Anaphase**

Centrosomes Spindle

Homologous chromosomes separate

Sister chromatids remain attached

3. Meiosis

In this process, the cell divides twice. This is used when the entire organism needs to reproduce. It is used to reproduce four sex cells or gametes instead of just two cells.

The new cells contain only half of the DNA or deoxyribonucleic acid of the original cell Hence, the cells produced through meiosis are called haploids. They help produce the variety of life on Earth. Meiosis allows new genetic combinations to take place.

Cells are made up of proteins and organelles. Organelles such as the nucleus and mitochondria perform amazing functions for the cells. The contents of human cells are kept together by a membrane.

The cell membranes contain cytoplasm and the nucleus. They act as compartments of the cells.

Cytoplasm is composed of cell structures that transform energy to let the cell function. The nucleus contains the genetic materials of the cells which control division and reproduction.

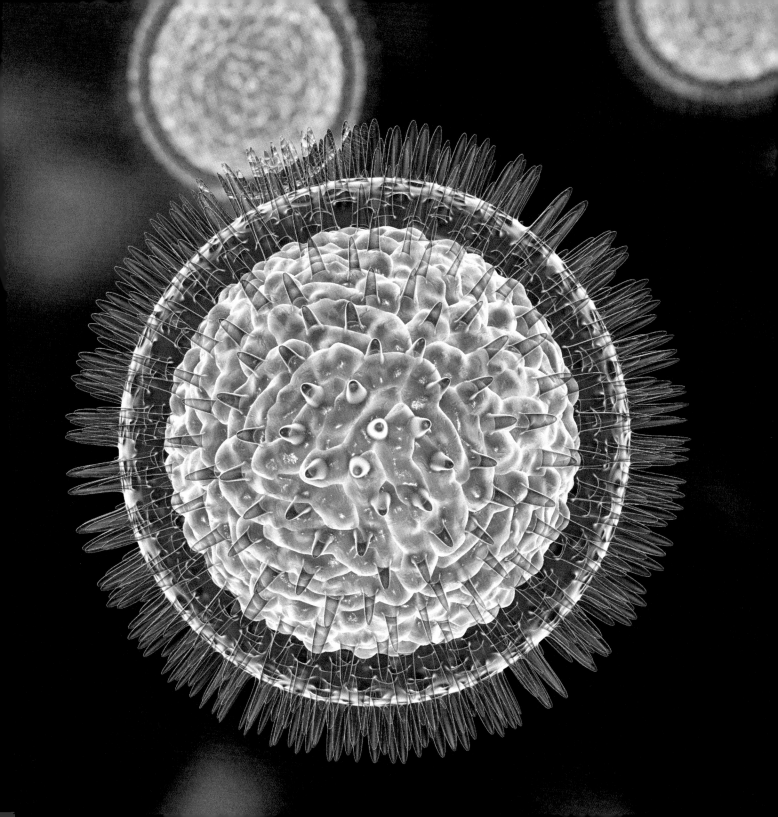

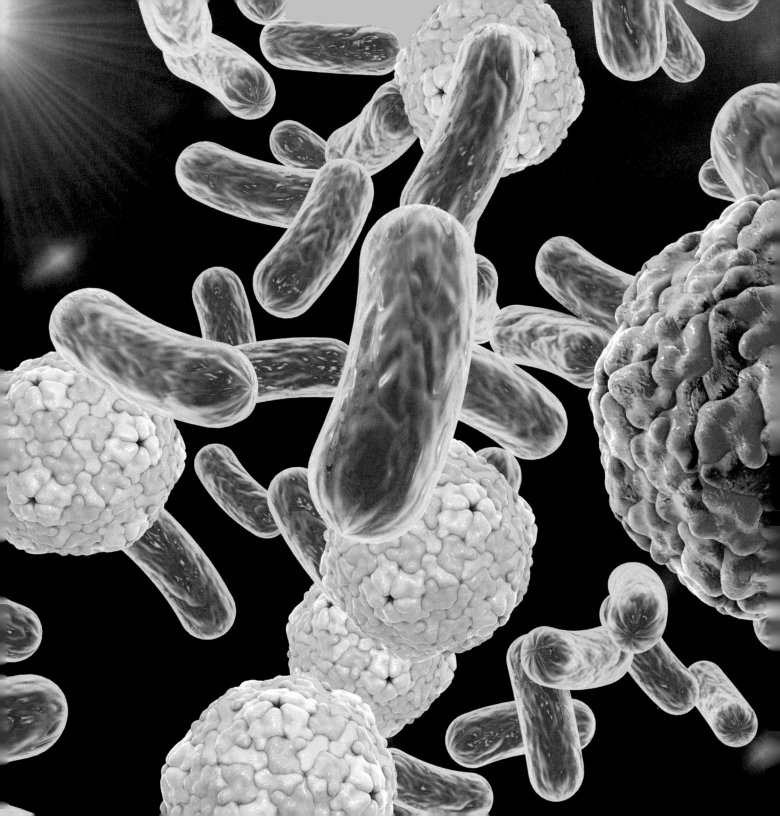

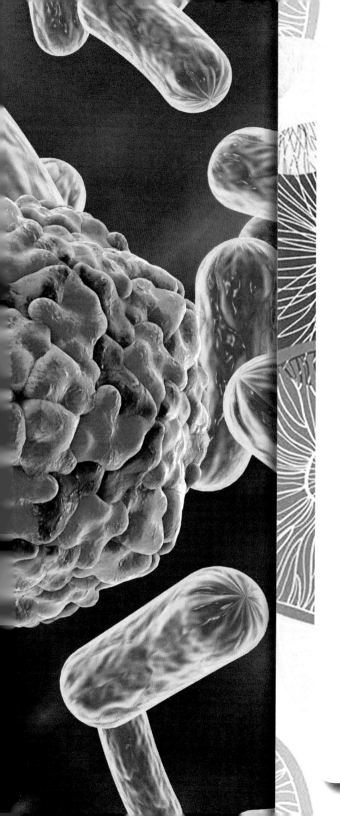

Living organisms exist because of the cells that make them up. These amazing tiny structures are the basics of life. Cells are very tiny but they make up organisms. Therefore, they can't just be ignored for they are the basis of life on Earth.